First Facts™

Holidays and Culture

Thanksgiving

A Day of Thanks

by Amanda Doering

Consultant:
Melodie Andrews, PhD
Associate Professor of Early American History
Minnesota State University, Mankato

Capstone
press®
Mankato, Minnesota

First Facts is published by Capstone Press,
151 Good Counsel Drive, P.O. Box 669, Mankato, Minnesota 56002.
www.capstonepress.com

Library of Congress Cataloging-in-Publication Data
Doering, Amanda.
    Thanksgiving : a day of thanks / by Amanda Doering.
    p. cm.—(First facts. Holidays and culture)
    Summary: "Describes the history and meaning of Thanksgiving and how it is celebrated
today"—Provided by publisher.
    Includes bibliographical references and index.
    ISBN-13: 978-0-7368-6399-5 (hardcover)
    ISBN-10: 0-7368-6399-0 (hardcover)
    1. Thanksgiving Day—Juvenile literature. I. Title. II. Series.
GT4975.D64 2007
394.2649—dc22   2006002951

Editorial Credits
Shari Joffe, editor; Biner Design, designer; Juliette Peters, set designer; Jo Miller, photo researcher;
    Scott Thoms, photo editor

Photo Credits
Capstone Press/Karon Dubke, 21
Corbis/Ariel Skelley, cover; Larry Williams, 4–5; Reuters/Shannon Stapleton, 16
Getty Images Inc./AFP/Brendan Smialowski, 20
The Granger Collection, New York, 8, 9
Grant Heilman Photography/Barry Runk, 15
Photodisc, 6
Shutterstock/Mark Aplet, 1
SuperStock, 10–11, 12, 13
Zuma Press/Icon SMI/James D. Smith, 18–19

Table of Contents

Celebrating Thanksgiving

Families gather at the dinner table. They **feast** on turkey, stuffing, cranberry sauce, and pumpkin pie until they can't eat any more. They are thankful for the delicious meal, their families, and their homes. It's Thanksgiving.

Fact!

Many people travel long distances to be with family on Thanksgiving. Thanksgiving is the busiest travel time of the year in the United States.

4

5

What Is Thanksgiving?

People in the United States celebrate Thanksgiving on the fourth Thursday of November. They remember how **Pilgrims** and American Indians shared a **harvest** feast long ago. Today, families have their own feast of thanks on Thanksgiving.

Fact!

American Indians had feasts of thanksgiving long before the "First Thanksgiving" they shared with the Pilgrims in 1621.

Thanksgiving History

The Pilgrims traveled from England to America in 1620. Their first winter in America was hard. Many of them died.

American Indians helped the Pilgrims plant crops in the spring. In the fall, there was a large harvest. The Pilgrims and Indians shared a feast.

Food at the 1621 Feast

Some of the foods at the 1621 feast were different from what we eat today. The Pilgrims and Indians ate deer. They ate wild birds such as turkey, swan, duck, or goose. They probably also ate fish and eels. There were no potatoes or yams. These foods had not yet been brought to New England.

A National Holiday

By the late 1700s, many Americans held a yearly day of thanks. Thanksgiving became an **official** holiday in many states in the 1800s.

Thanksgiving became a national holiday in 1863. In 1941, Congress decided Thanksgiving would be on the fourth Thursday of November.

13

Food Today

The **traditional** Thanksgiving meal includes turkey with stuffing and potatoes or yams. Turkey is served in honor of the feast that the Pilgrims and Indians shared.

Cranberry sauce and pumpkin pie are also favorite dishes. Cranberries and pumpkins are both foods the Pilgrims and Indians ate in the 1600s.

Fact!
Many families create new traditions by adding their own dishes to their Thanksgiving meal. Some people eat Chinese, Italian, or Mexican food. Some even order pizza.

Macy's Parade

Thousands of people line the streets of New York City on Thanksgiving morning. They are waiting to see Macy's Thanksgiving Day Parade.

Giant balloons float between the tall buildings. Singers and dancers entertain the crowd. All across the country, families enjoy this parade on television.

Thanksgiving Day Football

   As time goes on, families find new ways to give thanks and enjoy Thanksgiving. One recent tradition is football games. People watch the games before or after their meal. It's another way for families and friends to spend time together on Thanksgiving.

Amazing Holiday Story!

Every year, the president of the United States saves a turkey from becoming Thanksgiving dinner. This turkey will live the rest of its life on a farm. People can help name this turkey. They can vote for a name on the White House Web site.

Hands On: "Hand-Made" Turkey

The turkey is a symbol of Thanksgiving. Trace your hands and feet to make this turkey.

What You Need
pencil
red, orange, brown, and
 yellow construction paper
scissors
glue
medium-sized googly eyes or
 a black marker

What You Do
1. With a pencil, trace each of your feet on brown construction paper. Use a scissors to cut out the tracings.
2. Glue the two foot tracings together, spreading them slightly apart at the bottom. The narrow part at the top will be the turkey's head. The wider part will be the turkey's body.
3. Trace your hands on pieces of red, orange, and yellow construction paper. Cut out the tracings.
4. Glue these "feathers" behind the turkey's head and body.
5. Glue googly eyes on your turkey or draw eyes in with a black marker.
6. Cut a wattle out of red construction paper and glue it where the turkey's chin should be.
7. Cut feet and a beak out of orange or yellow construction paper. Glue them on your turkey.

Glossary

feast (FEEST)—to eat a large meal; a large, fancy meal for a lot of people on a special occasion.

harvest (HAR-vist)—crops that have been gathered in after they are ripe

official (uh-FISH-uhl)—approved by those in authority

Pilgrims (PIL-gruhms)—the people who left England, came to North America for religious freedom, and founded Plymouth Colony in 1620

traditional (truh-DISH-uhn-uhl)—handed down over the years

Read More

Harte, May. *Thanksgiving.* My Library of Holidays. New York: PowerKids Press, 2004.

Haugen, Brenda. *Thanksgiving.* Holidays and Celebrations. Minneapolis: Picture Window Books, 2004.

Kessel, Joyce K. *Squanto and the First Thanksgiving.* On My Own Holidays. Minneapolis: Carolrhoda Books, 2004.

Internet Sites

FactHound offers a safe, fun way to find Internet sites related to this book. All of the sites on FactHound have been researched by our staff.

Here's how:

1. Visit *www.facthound.com*

2. Choose your grade level.

3. Type in this book ID **0736863990** for age-appropriate sites. You may also browse subjects by clicking on letters, or by clicking on pictures and words.

4. Click on the **Fetch It** button.

FactHound will fetch the best sites for you!

Index